Be Aware of the footprints you
Leave Behind
"The Next Level Celebration"
Between Mortar and Miracles:
A Woman's Triumph in Construction"

© 2023 by Angela Boone
All rights reserved
The first edition printed in 2024
Printed in the United States of America

Library of Congress Cataloging-in-Publication Data

Book Cover Design by Angela Boone

CONTENT

Overview

Be Aware of the Footprints You Leave Behind- "The Next Level Celebration"

Embark on a journey that will redefine your perception of success and empowerment. Always, "Be Aware of the Footprints You Leave Behind – The Next Level Celebration" moves into the transformative power of wisdom, knowledge, and understanding rooted in the power of God. This book illuminates how you can overcome any challenge that stands in your path by integrating faith and scripture into every facet of daily life, goal setting, business ventures, and educational pursuits. Bear in mind the profound truth: "Without faith put into action, it remains dormant." (Referencing James 2:20&26).

Introduction

An Unexpected Sequel

The birth of the first book, "Faith Cometh by Hearing, The Celebration," was a testimony of perseverance. It was the story of a woman's will against the odds, of a single mother navigating the male-dominated construction industry, an industry that wasn't kind or forgiving. Yet, it was more than just a story of challenges; it was a testament to the belief in God, the human spirit, and the quiet power of faith.

When the ink dried on the last page of that first book, there was an overwhelming sense of completion. The journey had been long, and the road was often tricky, but I had traveled it and had penned down the legacy of those four ear-shattering decades.

The day my father held the first copy of "Faith Cometh by Hearing, The Celebration," he looked at me with those deep, discerning eyes and said, "Where is the rest of the story? There's a second book here."

At that moment, I was puzzled. What more was there to say? Hadn't I poured my heart out? Wasn't this narrative all-inclusive of my experiences?

Time has a beautiful way of clarifying things. As the days turned into months and the months into years, I began to understand what my father had intuitively seen. The first book, in its essence, was a story of struggle, strength, and triumph. But life doesn't stop after a victory; it continues, often presenting new challenges and opportunities. I realized that while I had captured the trials of the past, a whole world of experiences, insights, and revelations had transformed me and how I viewed the construction industry in the time since. I realized the story was ready for its next chapter.

" Be Aware of the Footprints You Leave Behind' 'The Next Celebration" continues that story, but it's more than just a sequel. It reflects on how the industry has evolved, how perspectives have shifted, and how some things remain timeless despite change. It's a celebration of lessons learned and wisdom gained.

Trials and tribulations never genuinely cease. They merely transform, and in their transformation, they gift us a new lens through which to view the world. The construction sites, blueprints, and machinery are all the same, but I stand in their midst a changed woman with deeper insights and a broader perspective.

With this book, I invite you to walk with me through this new landscape to understand not just the challenges of the past but also the promises and potential of the present and future and to "Be Aware of the Footprints You Leave Behind."

It is important to recognize that every story, no matter how complete it may seem, always has another chapter waiting to be written.

As you turn the pages, know that this isn't just a story of an industry or a profession. It's a testament to the enduring spirit of humanity, the faith that sustains us, and the belief that our core values and beliefs can remain steadfast even in the face of change.

I carved out a space for myself in the raw, rugged landscapes of construction sites, where the elaborate musical composition of a full orchestra of power tools and machinery paints a typically masculine portrait. As a woman navigating a male-dominated realm like construction, my journey has been anything but conventional. My armor? An unwavering faith that acted as the compass guiding me through each challenge and the ancient wisdom contained within the Word of God.

"Be Aware of the Footprints You Leave Behind: "The Next Level Celebration" is not a short lyric to my experiences but a testament to the power of faith when pitted against seemingly hopeless odds. It's about understanding that foundations in buildings and life are built brick by brick, prayer by prayer. The spiritual scaffolding I've erected over the years has given me the strength and the capacity to withstand and thrive where few women have ventured.

In these pages, I hope to inspire you. Whether you're a woman trying to break barriers in a traditionally male field or anyone feeling out of place in unfamiliar territory, let this book serve as a reminder: with faith as your ally, guided by the timeless teachings of the scriptures, there's no challenge too vast, no skyscraper too tall. Emerge yourself and witness how, when faith meets determination, any structure, no matter how grand, is possible.

Welcome to "Be Aware of the Footprints You Leave Behind.", The Next Celebration".

Chapter 1
Four Decades of Divine Blueprint

My earliest memories in the construction industry are vivid and filled with a sense of purpose—the hustle of machines, the throbbing hammering, and the scent of fresh earth. Four decades ago, I was that wide-eyed young woman stepping into a world dominated by the fullness of male voices, where steel-toed boots were far more common than high heels. But within this expanse of concrete, steel, and dirt, I found a purpose and a partnership with a divine force that guided me through every step.

Back then, whispers of doubt were not uncommon, and some would murmur, "She's too young." "What does she know about construction?" Others would scoff. The truth? At that time, not as much as I would have liked. But I made up for what I lacked in knowledge, determination, an unquenchable appetite to learn, and a huge mountain of faith that God had set me on this path for a reason.

Every day was a new lesson. The construction site became both my classroom and my sanctuary. From understanding the intricacies of design to managing the complex and sometimes unpleasant conditions of the site, every challenge was an opportunity for growth. But more than the technicalities, the field's complex wisdom truly molded me. The art of negotiation, the knack of leadership, the finesse of diplomacy, and the courage to stand up in a room full of doubters were lessons no classroom could ever impart.

Over the years, I've had the privilege to work alongside some incredible minds. Many were supportive, but some questioned my abilities because of my gender. In those trying moments, my faith acted as my compass. It whispered words of encouragement when the world wanted to drown me in doubt. It reminded me that God's wisdom was far more profound than the limitations placed upon me by certain groups of people. And with each passing project, every completed building, I silenced the skeptics not with words but with the quality of my work and the depth of my commitment.

Today, 40 years later, when I look back, I see more than just structures and blueprints. I see a tapestry of experiences woven together with threads of challenges, successes, failures, and divine interventions. The journey has been anything but linear. But every twist and turn was supported by the love for my craft and the unwavering belief that God was guiding me through it all.

Now, as a seasoned professional in the construction industry, I carry the weight of experience, an experience that books couldn't teach, an experience that was earned brick by brick, day by day, on the construction site with the omnipresent guidance of God.

To every young woman or anyone looking to carve their path in a field dominated by skepticism and stereotypes, remember this: real wisdom often comes from the unlikeliest of classrooms. And when paired with faith, it becomes an unstoppable force capable of building structures and legacies.

Chapter 2
Building Integrity Among Baseless Whispers

The construction site is the humming of machines, the clinking of tools, and the purposeful chatter of workers coordinating tasks. But, sometimes, it was the quieter whispers that echoed the loudest. Stories that carried insinuations were more piercing than the loudest drill.

"You know why she got that contract, right?"

It's ironic how, in a world of tangible, solid structures, the most intangible of rumors can attempt to shake one's foundation. There was no lack of naysayers who sought to undermine my accomplishments with baseless allegations when faced with a woman's success in a male-dominated industry. "She must've slept with someone at the top," they'd insinuate with a knowing smirk as if that was the only explanation for my achievements.

I won't deny the sting of such words. To see years of sweat, determination, and countless hours of learning and honing my craft reduced to a baseless rumor was painful. But in the face of such adversity, there were two pillars I leaned on: the integrity of my work and my unwavering faith in God's wisdom.

Every contract I secured and every project I undertook was a testament to my dedication, skill, and unwavering commitment to excellence. While my belittlers whispered behind closed doors, I let the quality of my work speak for itself. Each structure that bore my signature was a clear message to the world: I earned my place, brick by brick, blueprint by blueprint.

God's wisdom was my daily support. In moments of self-doubt, when the insinuations threatened to cloud my vision, I sought refuge in prayer. I remembered that God's plan for me was more significant than the confines of societal gossip. I leaned on scriptures that spoke to my integrity and the strength to stand tall through the storms.

Over time, I realized that while I couldn't control the whispers, I had complete control over my reaction to them. Instead of constantly retreating or needing to defend my honor, I poured my energy into my passion. I helped build physical structures and monuments of perseverance against the deceitful, baseless chatter.

It's essential to understand that rumors and whispers often arise from insecurity, an inability to accept change, or the rise of those who challenge the status quo. But these should never discourage one from their path. My journey in the construction industry, with God as my guide, taught me this: When faced with baseless allegations, let the integrity of your work be your loudest rebuttal.

To anyone walking a path laden with skepticism and ill-intentioned rumors, always remember: Build your legacy with such authenticity and dedication that it towers over and silences the whispers of doubt. Let your work and God's guiding wisdom be your vindication.

Chapter 3
From Novice to Maverick: Navigating the Shades of Envy

After four decades in the construction industry, from a young enthusiast trying to find her footing among the giants, I evolved into a seasoned professional. This maverick had carved out a niche and made a mark. With age and experience on my side, the path ahead would be no emotions of those determined to undermine me. But life, as always, had its surprises.

I had ascended the ranks, not just in terms of experience but also in the respect I commanded. Yet, just as in my youth, there was a presence, a shadow, trying to block my achievements. This time, it wasn't the inexperience or age working against me. Instead, it was someone who had walked alongside me in this journey, a fellow veteran.

This person had been there as long as I had, watching, often from the sidelines, as I made audacious moves, took calculated risks, and celebrated victories. But now, their position was to challenge my entrepreneurial judgment and set up roadblocks, placing hurdles in my path and hoping to watch me falter.

But why? What drives a seasoned professional to pull the rug from under a peer?

It took time and reflection to realize that their actions were not a reflection of my abilities but a mirror of their insecurities. Over the years, I have transformed every challenge into an opportunity, grown from every failure, and, most importantly, never let the skeptics define my narrative. However, this person, despite their experience, perhaps felt overshadowed and threatened by the innovation my team and I brought to each project.

They openly displayed strategies; from misplacing vital documents to trying to sow seeds of discord within my team to whispering doubts into the ears of our clients, they tried it all. Even though these tactics were designed by then to destroy what my team and I had built, they only fueled my passion.

Drawing from the lessons of the past and with the grace of God's wisdom, I chose to combat this not with confrontation but with competence. I intensified my focus on team unity, ensuring we were all aligned in our goals and trust for one another. And above all, we leaned on the strength of our portfolio, letting the quality of our work be our shield against any sabotage.

As time went on, the attempts to undermine us became more desperate and, in that desperation, more transparent. Stakeholders, clients, and even some of her allies began to recognize the game for what it was. And as the truth unfolded, her influence disappeared.

This chapter of my journey reminded me that challenges in one's professional path aren't merely about capability but often about the human implications of jealousy, insecurity, and competition. Yet, no matter the source of the challenge, the response should always be grounded in integrity, perseverance, and unwavering belief in one's purpose.

Ultimately, the story isn't about those who try to pull you down but about how you rise, time and time again, fortified by experience and guided by divine wisdom.

Chapter 4
Standing Tall in the Shadows of Doubt

Forty years. Over four decades in the construction industry, the landscape has changed in countless ways: new technologies, evolving techniques, and a slow but evident shift towards a more excellent practice or policy of providing equal access to opportunities and resources for people who would otherwise be excluded. Yet, one stubbornly consistent aspect: the doubters, the skeptics, and those wishing to see one falter is still alive.

From the fresh-faced novice, eager to make their mark but misguided in their methods, to the seasoned professional, set in their ways and unwilling to acknowledge the winds of change, I've encountered skepticism from every corner. It's perplexing and, at times, disheartening. After all, why would someone with such a vast experience, with a portfolio of accomplishments as expansive as the horizon, still face such undermining?

The young may see my tenure as challenging; in their zeal to climb and conquer, their quickest way up the ladder. Their inexperience closes their eyes to the reality that success isn't about pulling others down but about lifting oneself and those around them.

On the other hand, seasoned professionals who have witnessed this industry's evolution sometimes see my continued success as a mirror, reflecting their own insecurities and unfulfilled ambitions. Rather than embracing change and growth, they find comfort in resisting, often by attempting to undermine those who represent that change.

Over the years, I've felt the subtle nudges designed to trip me up. Contracts are mysteriously going away, last-minute changes intended to derail, and hidden obstacles placed with the hope of witnessing my stumble. It wasn't just me; my team and extended family also faced these challenges. The goal was clear: to set us up for failure, to create a narrative that, despite decades in the business, we didn't have what it took.

But why? Why is it this constant need to see me falter?

The answer is complex and layered in human emotions and psychology. Sometimes, it's pure envy and resentment toward someone who has achieved what others only dreamed of. Other times, it's fear—the fear of change, the fear of being overshadowed, or the fear of an evolving industry that doesn't have space for outdated mindsets. And for some, it's a misguided strategy, a belief that undermining competitors is the path to success.

Yet, in these challenges, I found my strength. Each attempt to destabilize me only rooted me firmer in my convictions. With God's guidance, each challenge became an opportunity, a chance to prove, yet again, that I was here because of merit, hard work, and an unyielding passion for my craft.

In this journey, I've learned invaluable lessons:
1.   Doubters will always exist, irrespective of one's achievements.
2.   It's not the external voices of skepticism that define us but our internal convictions.
3.   The true mark of success isn't in never facing challenges but in rising, time and again, despite them.

To every entrepreneur and every dreamer facing whispers of doubt, remember this: Your legacy will be defined not by the number of challenges you face but by the number of times you rise above them. Stand tall, lean on your faith, and let every attempt to undermine you be a stepping-stone to greater heights.

Chapter 5
Foundations of Faith - Walls of Prejudice

In a rapidly changing, adapting, and evolving world, certain prejudices remain rooted deep, creating cracks and crevices in the structure of our society. Four decades in the construction industry, and while I have witnessed immense growth, innovations, and transformations, the shadows of racism persist, casting a dark cloud.

Being an African American woman at the helm of my own company in this space isn't just about navigating the complexities of construction but also constantly dismantling the barriers of bias and prejudice. It's a dual challenge: confronting the already entrenched gender biases and battling the undercurrents of racial discrimination.

There have been moments, more than I'd have liked, where my peers questioned my capability, not because of my decisions or my skills but purely because of my skin color. Whispers in corners, subtle microaggressions, or outright confrontations – racism donned many masks, each trying to belittle, undermine, intimidate.

Why? Perhaps it's fear – fear of change, fear of losing power or status, or maybe just an irrational bias cultivated over generations. But the 'why' becomes secondary when faced with the 'how' – how does one persevere in such adversity?

Here, faith becomes the bedrock. As the scripture reminds us, "Now faith is the substance of things hoped for, the evidence of things not seen" (Hebrews 11:1). As the sun dawns, heralding a new day every morning, I seek God's wisdom. It's not merely about asking for strength to face the challenges but seeking discernment to understand and navigate the maze of prejudice without losing one's essence.

The scripture also tells us, "If any of you lacks wisdom, you should ask God, who gives generously to all without finding fault, and it will be given to you" (James 1:5). This verse isn't just words to me; it's a lived experience. Every project, every meeting, every challenge, I've leaned into God's wisdom, often finding paths I hadn't perceived, solutions that seemed elusive, and patience when it was most needed.

Faith isn't passive; it's active, vibrant, and pulsating with life. It's faith that has given me the courage to stand tall while in the middle of derogatory comments, to respond with grace to blatant racism, and to lead with compassion even when met with hostility. Now, I want you to know that when met with derogatory comments and blatant racism, I am not always led with compassion or quiet to what is or was said; I have lashed out. Is it wise? No, not all the time; however, sometimes it must happen.

That is why faith, combined with determination, has not only carved a niche for me in the construction industry, but I hope to have paved the way for many more to walk unburdened in this field.

To every woman and individual facing the chains of prejudice, remember this: barriers are external, but strength, wisdom, and faith blossom from within. Keep them alive and burning, and let them be your guiding light. The construction industry, like any other, will evolve. And while the walls of racism may not crumble immediately, with faith and perseverance, we'll indeed lay bricks of change, one day at a time.

Chapter 6
Echoes from the Elevator

The construction site is a dynamic entity. It breathes, evolves, and transforms daily. Among the clatter of machinery and the hum of activity, each day is unique, presenting a picture of ever-changing scenarios. However, some constants remain—the trials we face, the judgments we encounter, and the prejudice that lingers even in all the progress.

It was an ordinary day, or so it seemed, when I crossed paths with the woman in question. The sunlight cascaded down on the newly laid bricks and reflected off hard hats. Up to that point, my day had been filled with the usual meetings, site inspections, and quick chit-chats with workers. And then, out of the blue, a seemingly fleeting interaction left a lasting mark on my mind.

She had an air of distinction about her, releasing uneasiness in her stride. Accompanied by one of our project managers, they seemed engrossed in conversation. When the project manager spotted me and paused to converse, I detected a sense of impatience in the woman's eyes, as if our interaction hindered her busy schedule. Her mood was visible, yet I paid it no mind.

However, destiny, or perhaps just the design of the job site, brought us together again at the elevators. The layout of the elevator system at the time of construction was second nature to regulars yet perplexing to outsiders. Recognizing her bewilderment, I stepped in to assist. My natural inclination to help always overpowers any reservations I may hold.

It was then that her true colors emerged. She unveiled her title, the 'Director of ABC company,' with a hint of arrogance. She felt her attire was beneath her stature, and she wasn't shy about vocalizing it. But her insinuation about the Zoom call and the jab about my 'pay grade,' which she knew nothing about, revealed the depth of what she felt was her self-importance.

Silently, I reflected on the situation. She judged me based on appearance, unaware that I, too, was a force to be reckoned with in this industry. I could have unveiled my title, stood my ground, and enlightened her about her company's missteps. Yet, I chose humility—not because I felt lesser, but because I believe in the power of silent strength.

We often encounter individuals who are blinded by their privilege or status, so they say, overlook the worth of those around them. But if the world of construction has taught me anything, it's that the strength of a structure isn't evident from its facade; it lies within. Similarly, our worth isn't defined by titles or perceptions. Our actions and ability to rise above prejudice define it.

In the construction world, as in life, every brick, every beam, and every worker plays a pivotal role. Each person has a story, a legacy, and a worth. Encounters like these serve as a reminder to always look beyond the surface, never underestimate anyone, and stand tall, not in arrogance, but in humility and strength.

Chapter 7
Foundations Tested: The Union Challenge

In the vast expanse of the construction landscape, cranes touching the skies and deep foundations dug daily, I spotted a golden opportunity: launching a second construction company, not just any company, but a union one. I was excited at the chance to elevate my business while supporting the many union workers who found themselves without work.

The vision was crystal clear. This venture was not merely a business expansion; it was a chance to merge my primary company's precision, dedication, and values with the experience of seasoned union workers. A marriage of strengths, if you will. And with the number of union workers laid off, it felt like a calling. Here was a chance to provide jobs, ensure livelihoods, and create a harmonious blend of experience and passion.

But as the bricks started laying, cracks began appearing.

With their vast experience, the seasoned union workers brought something unexpected to the table: a lowering of the standards I held so dear. It was as if my company's meticulously crafted reputation, built over decades, was at the mercy of a sledgehammer. For all their experience, the union workers were working with a different rulebook that didn't align with the values and standards I had cultivated.

So far, my first and only union project has witnessed a lack of the precision and passion I deemed non-negotiable. When confronted, a few of them shrugged it off, stating this work was "beneath them." Their pride overshadowed their commitment to excellence.

It was a challenging period. My core team and I faced the challenges of integrating new members and safeguarding the company's hard-earned reputation. Letting some union workers go was a tough decision, given that the company's initial purpose was to provide employment. But the stakes were too high; the very essence of my company was under threat.

During this chaos, I questioned everything. The vision God had guided me toward seemed clouded and doubtful. Was this a test of faith? Or had I misread the signs? The sleepless nights, the second-guessing, and the emotional and mental toll pointed towards one overwhelming feeling: the urge to walk away from it all.

But I wasn't one to back down without a fight. Before making any drastic decisions, I sought a meeting with the union. The discussions were intense, filled with frustration, hope, and a desperate need for understanding. My goal was simple: realign the union's workers with the values and standards that took decades to establish.

While the road ahead with the union was still uncertain, the meeting served as a turning point. It reminded me of the challenges I had overcome, the barriers I had shattered, and the faith that had been my guiding light. Yet another hurdle, and with God's wisdom and my relentless spirit, I was determined to find a way through.

As a disclaimer, the union is a remarkable institution designed to assist those who might otherwise struggle to secure employment. Its establishment fosters collective strength, offers protection, and ensures equitable work opportunities for many. However, like any system, there are always those few who seek to exploit its structures for personal gain. It's crucial to recognize that when such manipulations go unchecked, they can diminish the union's effectiveness and betray the community it seeks to serve.

To every entrepreneur facing unforeseen challenges, remember this: setbacks are temporary, but the lessons learned and the strength gained are eternal. Hold onto your vision, stay anchored in your values, and let your faith guide you through the stormiest days.

Chapter 8
Unwrapping the Chocolate: Wisdom for the Next Generation

As the years have ticked by, the questions have become almost as predictable as the changing seasons. Young, bright-eyed entrepreneurs often approach me, brimming with ambition, asking, "What advice can you give to someone who wants to succeed like you in the business world?"

While I'm honored that my journey serves as an inspiration, I'm also keenly aware that the path to success isn't a one-size-fits-all formula. Yet, certain universal principles stand as steadfast as the most durable foundations we've built upon, principles that are essential for anyone aiming to thrive in any industry.

First and foremost, "Treat people how you want to be treated." Simple yet profound, this golden rule transcends business jargon and strategies, diving deep into the core of human interaction. Maintaining a sense of humanity can set you apart in an industry or a world that often prioritizes profits over people. Remember, businesses are built not just on balance sheets but on relationships—relationships with employees, vendors, clients, and even competitors. The respect and dignity you offer today may very well be the cornerstone of a partnership or opportunity tomorrow.

My second advice is, "Don't judge a book by its cover." It's easy to make assumptions based on appearances. In the male-dominated construction field, I've witnessed firsthand how detrimental such judgments can be. Stereotypes about gender, race, or even job roles can close our eyes to the talents and opportunities that stand right in front of us.

Think of life like a box of chocolates; you only know what's inside once you bite. A modest-looking truffle may hold the most exquisite filling, just as a seemingly unremarkable individual might possess untapped expertise or innovative ideas. Before jumping to conclusions based on superficial characteristics, dig deeper.

Which brings me to my next point: "Look beyond the surface." If you're genuinely keen on understanding a person's worth or the value of a company, learn as much about their history as you can. Research how they got to where they are today. The road to success is often paved with challenges, innovations, and critical decisions that reveal much about one's character and capabilities.

Just as I navigated through prejudices and obstacles, you'll find that many successful people have stories that serve not just as an account of their achievements but also as a testament to their passion to succeed, creativity, and ethics. Understanding this journey offers a far more comprehensive picture than any judgment can.

So, to the younger generation eager to carve out your path in the complex business world, remember: your journey will be uniquely your own, but let it be guided by principles that are as timeless as they are universal.

Value people, keep an open mind, and always seek a deeper story. As you journey through your own 'box of chocolates' of experiences, you may find that the most rewarding flavors come from the most unexpected quarters.

Chapter 9
Bridges to the Future - Paving the Way for the Next Generation

In the vast tapestry of life, we each stand as a unique thread, weaving stories and crafting legacies. As I look back over the decades, the patchwork of my journey stands in vivid colors, each hue representing challenges faced, broken barriers, and milestones achieved. On the wall of my study are framed testimonials, newspaper and coffee table book articles, and awards, which speak volumes of my recognition. Yet, they serve as more than just accolades of past achievements. They are stepping stones, bridges to the future, that the next generation can confidently traverse.

The awards, ranging from industry recognitions to resolutions from the city council, came with significant trials. The journey of entrepreneurship and construction has its pitfalls, notably financial hurdles. There were times when the weight of financial obligations threatened to bring everything, I had built crumbling down. But adversity has a purpose. It introduces us to ourselves, pushing us to think outside the box and compelling us to find creative solutions when traditional routes fail.

During one of the most trying times, I challenged myself to innovate financial avenues, reinvent my business model, leverage assets in other ways, and collaborate with stakeholders to ensure a win-win situation. My model was straightforward: breaking financial barriers was not about having endless resources but about using what one had.

Yet, with all the successes, there was an internal question that I struggled with. What was the purpose of these awards? Why had my journey been sprinkled with so many accolades? Was it a reflection of my past or a signpost pointing toward the future?

I remember one quiet evening; after another eventful day, I found myself in solitude. With a heavy heart, I turned to the divine, seeking answers. "God," I yelled, "Why? What is the significance of these awards? What is the message you are conveying?"

Though not audible, the response was solid in every fiber of my being. It was as if a gentle voice echoed within me, saying, "These are not just recognition of what you have done, but a roadmap of where I'm taking you. Each award and testimonial is a testament to your journey and a bridge to where the next generation needs to go. You are laying the foundations, paving the paths, building the bridges for them to travel confidently."

This revelation transformed my perspective. It was no longer about personal glory or individual achievement. It was about legacy, about ensuring that the future generation has a path forward and bridges they can confidently cross. Every project I undertook, every structure I built, was with this renewed vision - to not just create for the present but to pave the way for the future.

Bridges, after all, are symbols of connections. They link the past with the future, the known with the unknown. As I move forward, I do so with a profound sense of responsibility, knowing that I am not just building for today but for generations yet unborn.

Chapter 10
Cementing Bonds: The Blueprint of Meaningful Relationships in Construction

In the grand architecture of the construction industry, while beams, bricks, and bolts play their undeniable role, it's the invisible threads of relationships that truly hold the structure together. The landscape of construction isn't merely built upon mortar and machines but on meetings, memories, and mutual respect.

To a novice, the industry might seem solely about tangible outputs: skyscrapers piercing the heavens, bridges spanning vast expanses, or homes echoing with warmth. However, those who investigate deeper, those who really succeed, know that these landmarks are just the tip of the iceberg. Beneath them lies a complex network of relationships and networks, each junction holding a story, an opportunity, a lesson.

One of the earliest lessons I learned was the power of meaningful relationships. Not the superficial, transactional interactions that are all too common, but genuine connections built over shared values, mutual respect, and consistent communication. Whether it was with suppliers ensuring the best materials, contractors executing visions to perfection, or clients entrusting us with their dreams, every relationship was an investment.

And in this intricate dance of interactions, two steps stood out: Networking and Follow-up.

Networking: Laying the First Brick

Every successful skyscraper starts with a single brick, and in the realm of relationships, that brick is networking. However, effective networking goes beyond just exchanging business cards at events. It's about curiosity, understanding, and genuine interest. It's about finding common ground, shared visions, and potential synergies.

Over the years, many of the projects that defined our portfolio had their genesis in the most unexpected networking moments. Casual conversations over coffee, shared panel discussions, and even chance airport encounters turned into collaborations of a lifetime. The key was always to approach every interaction with an open mind and heart.

Follow-up: The Reinforcing Steel

If networking is the first brick, consistent follow-up is the steel reinforcement that gives a relationship its strength and durability. A connection, no matter how promising, can easily fade away during our busy daily business if not nurtured with care.

I recall numerous instances where opportunities seemed elusive, with doors seemingly shut. However, persistence, paired with genuine intent, often turned the tides. It wasn't about pushing aggressively but about reminding, updating, and showcasing value consistently. Many companies I yearned to work with became long-term partners, not because of a single impactful pitch but due to the continuous echo of sincere follow-ups and outstanding work when the bid was won.

The art of following up isn't just about reminders for potential business. It's about sharing updates, celebrating milestones, and even sometimes just sending a note to check-in. These gestures, small yet significant, keep the relationship alive and evolving.

In conclusion, as you navigate the vast and intricate world of construction, remember that the most majestic of structures are as much about their hidden foundations as they are about their visible magnificence. Cultivate relationships with the same precision and care as you would a landmark project. Because, in the end, it's these bonds, these interconnected networks of trust and collaboration, that truly shape the skyline of success.

Chapter 11
Foundations of Relationship-Building
A Blueprint for Success

In the multifaceted world of construction, as in any industry, the structures we erect are not just made of bricks and mortar, steel and concrete. They're built on something even more foundational: relationships. Just as a building requires a solid foundation to stand tall and withstand external pressures, businesses thrive on the bedrock of genuine connections, consistent networking, and diligent follow-up.

The Art of Authenticity:

Whether you're meeting a contractor, a potential partner, or a client, the key is to be genuine. Authenticity is unmatchable. People can sense when you are genuinely interested in them or their project and when you're just going through the motions. Remember, in any industry, business is not just about transactions; it's about trust. And trust is cultivated when you engage authentically.

Active Listening:

One of the most profound ways to connect with others is by truly listening. Instead of preparing your next statement while the other person is speaking, take the time to understand their perspective. This shows respect and can provide invaluable insights, whether about a project's specific requirements or broader industry trends.

Networking is Nurturing:

Networking isn't just about collecting business cards or adding LinkedIn connections. It's about nurturing relationships. Attend industry events, participate in workshops, or simply set up regular coffee meetings with peers. The construction industry, vast as it is, thrives on the collective knowledge and collaboration of its members.

The Power of Follow-Up:

A meeting or a casual conversation at an event may go well, but it's the follow-up that often seals the deal. It shows your commitment and genuine interest. I've secured countless projects, not necessarily because I had the most impressive pitch initially, but because I stayed consistent in my communications, showing potential clients or partners that I was genuinely invested in collaboration.

Flexibility and Adaptability:

While consistency in follow-ups is essential, adaptability is equally important. Understand that every individual and company has its own working style and pace. Sometimes, a deal might take longer than expected to materialize. Patience, combined with a willingness to adapt, can be the key to long-term partnerships.

Reciprocity:

A relationship is a two-way street. Offer help when you can, even if it's not immediately beneficial for you. Whether it's sharing a contact, providing industry insights, or lending equipment when someone else breaks down, these gestures of goodwill are remembered and often reciprocated.

Celebrate Successes:

Celebrate when a project is completed or an important milestone is reached. It's a testament to the collaboration and strengthens the bond between the parties involved. Such moments, when acknowledged and celebrated, foster a sense of team spirit and camaraderie.

In an age of digital communications that are omnipresent, the essence of genuine human connection remains paramount. Whether you're in construction, tech, healthcare, or any other industry, the principles of building and nurturing relationships remain consistent. As I've learned over the years, the dividends these relationships pay in terms of opportunities, collaborations, and growth are invaluable.

So, as you lay down bricks or draft business plans, remember to also consistently lay down the blocks of trust, understanding, and collaboration. Because, at the end of the day, it's not just about constructing buildings or businesses but about building bridges of genuine, lasting relationships.

Chapter 12
The Pillars of Trust: Transparency, Integrity, and Authenticity

In the bustling realm of business, especially in industries as intricate and interwoven as construction, one truth remains unwavering: relationships are paramount. However, relationships, much like the structures we build, must rest on a solid foundation to withstand the test of time and trials. The cornerstones of this foundation are trust and transparency.

The Currency of Trust:

Trust is a currency that, once spent, is difficult to earn back. In an environment where teams need to work closely, where the safety and integrity of a project are at stake, and where reputation travels faster than light, trust is not just desirable – it's indispensable. From securing contracts to fostering long-term collaborations, the level of trust you build directly correlates with your professional trajectory.

The Clarity of Transparency:

Transparency is akin to a clear, unblemished windowpane through which stakeholders can view your operations, ethos, and values. It means sharing not just your successes but also your challenges and how you plan to address them. It involves open communication, setting clear expectations, and, most importantly, being honest when things don't go as planned. In doing so, you're not showcasing vulnerability but rather strength and accountability.

The Stain of Deception:

Conversely, deceit acts like a dark stain on this windowpane. The moment someone is found to be dishonest, manipulative, or bigoted, the murkiness clouds all interact, past and future.

Whether it's an exaggerated claim, a hidden flaw, or a prejudiced comment, the damage is done.

In my journey, I have encountered individuals, both young and old, who, under the guise of partnership or collaboration, harbored ulterior motives or bigoted beliefs. Once such a disposition comes to light, trust is not just broken; it shatters. While professional interactions may continue out of necessity or contractual obligations, the previous warmth, openness, and genuine collaboration are replaced with caution, skepticism, and distance.

Rebuilding Broken Bridges:

While rebuilding trust will become difficult, it's not impossible. However, it requires consistent efforts, genuine remorse, and tangible actions to demonstrate change. But why tread this difficult path when one can operate with integrity from the beginning?

Navigating the Landscape:

As you navigate the industry, be it construction or any other, be aware of the footprints you leave behind. While skills, expertise, and experience are critical, it's your reputation, built on transparency and trustworthiness, that often precedes you. Guard it zealously. The relationships you nurture, grounded in honesty and mutual respect, will be your most significant assets, opening doors and creating opportunities beyond your imagination.

In the end, it's not just about erecting a large or massive structure or scaling corporate ladders but about constructing a legacy of integrity and authenticity. A legacy that, long after projects are completed, stands as a testament to your character, work ethic, and the relationships you've cherished and upheld.

Chapter 13
Beyond Assumptions: The Layers of Legacy

In a world quick to form opinions, where first impressions carry undue weight, the risk of overlooking an individual's depth and rich history is alarmingly high. Such surface judgments are not just shallow; they can be misleading and rob us of opportunities to truly connect and collaborate. My journey in the construction industry stands as a testament to the need to look beyond the apparent to understand a person's or company's history before jumping to conclusions.

From my early days managing large-scale projects to overseeing intricate elements of multi-billion-dollar programs, this journey has been nothing short of transformative. Each project, whether worth $400,000 or being part of a whopping 1.5-billion-dollar capital improvement venture, was a lesson, a stepping stone, and a testament to the multifaceted skills my team and I brought to the table.

Yet, like any seasoned traveler who knows that the journey is as important as the destination, I saw a niche that many overlooked—construction final cleaning. To the untrained eye, it might seem like a step-down, transitioning from high-profile project management to ensuring construction sites were spotless and ready for occupancy. But this couldn't be further from the truth.

In construction, as in life, it's the finishes and the final touches that often make all the difference. Imagine erecting a magnificent structure, only to falter at the final hurdle by failing to present it in its best light. Construction final cleaning is not just about cleanliness; it's about bringing a vision to completion, ensuring that every element, from the largest beam to the smallest corner, shines in its intended glory.

It's true; some raised eyebrows, questioning the shift from handling hefty projects to "merely cleaning up." Yet, these are the same individuals who miss a crucial point: no project, no matter how grand or well-executed, can be deemed complete without that final, immaculate touch. In essence, our contribution becomes the bridge between construction and commencement, between a site and a ready-to-use structure.

It's in these moments of doubt, when faced with superficial judgments that I'm reminded of a higher purpose and direction and an old adage that says, "***God doesn't call the qualified; He qualifies the called.***" It's a profound realization that our paths, however winding or unexpected, are part of a larger design, a design where each of us, with our unique skills and histories, has a role, a purpose, and a place.

In the grand tapestry of the construction world, every thread has its value, and every color has its significance. Instead of assuming a hue's worth based on its current position, see its origin and journey. You'll find stories of innovation, vision, and, most importantly, a commitment to excellence that transcends roles and titles.

So, the next time you encounter someone or something, pause before you label or judge. Understand the history, the journey, and the multitude of experiences that have shaped the present. For in understanding, we not only foster respect and collaboration but also open doors to unseen potentials and partnerships.

Chapter 14
The Layers Beneath the Surface
Why Knowing a Person's History Matters

The construction site is a canvas of moving parts, with each wheel in the machine being as vital as the next. In this landscape, judgments often fly as quickly as dust in the wind based on titles, tasks, or even the tools in one's hands. But while these quick assessments may offer a superficial understanding of a role or individual, they often miss the nuance, the depth, and the journey behind it all.

In my own trajectory, I started out as a project manager overseeing large projects. Over the years, my portfolio ranged from $400,000 contracts to involvement in a $1.5 billion capital improvement program. But as time passed, I recognized an under-served niche—construction final cleaning. To the casual observer or uninformed critic, this pivot might appear as a downgrade, a shift from the complex world of project management to 'merely' cleaning up after a project's completion.

Surface vs. Substance

This cursory judgment, however, couldn't be further from the truth. What many fail to grasp is the indispensable role that construction final cleaning plays in any project. A project cannot be considered complete, nor can it close, without this crucial step. The floors must be pristine, the windows must be spotless, and every surface must meet not just aesthetic standards but often regulatory ones as well. It's a specialization that demands its own set of skills, understanding, and management acumen.

The Role of Divine Guidance

I often say, "We're put where we're most needed, even if others can't see it." I know God guided me toward this niche for a reason, showing me the gaps that others couldn't see at the time or chose to ignore. Where some see a mop and bucket, I see an indispensable wheel in the lifecycle of construction, a vocation that's as noble as it is necessary.

The Importance of Knowing the Full Story

This leads to a crucial point—"*never assume someone's journey or worth based on the chapter you walk in on*." Just as you wouldn't judge a book solely by its cover or its ending, take the time to understand the complete story. Whether you're networking, negotiating contracts, or collaborating on a project, knowing the history behind the person or the role they're in now can offer invaluable insights. It provides context, enriches collaboration, and fosters a more inclusive environment.

People who understand my journey from project management to construction final cleaning see the logical evolution, the business acumen behind identifying a niche, and the dedication to fulfilling a vital need in the industry. That's a far cry from the presumption that we are 'just cleaners.'

A Testament to Adaptability and Vision

My background is not a tale of descent but one of adaptability, diversification, and filling a vital void in the industry. It's a story that should remind everyone to look deeper, to understand the myriad paths that can lead to success, and to respect the often-underestimated roles that are nonetheless crucial.

So, before passing judgments or making assumptions, take a step back. Understand the layers beneath the surface. Doing so not only enriches your own understanding but builds a culture of respect and collaboration, essential ingredients for any successful project, company, or career. And who knows? The insights gained from knowing someone's full story might just inspire your own next chapter.

Chapter 15
Beyond the Surface
Embracing the Depth of Experience

The world is often in a rush—a rush to categorize, to pigeonhole, and, sadly, to assume. In such a whirlwind, it's all too easy to make quick judgments based on the present, overlooking the rich tapestry of experiences and decisions that make up a person's journey. But the story of our evolution, the chapters we've written over years of hard work and determination, deserves more than a cursory glance. They warrant understanding and respect.

I began my professional odyssey in project management within the construction industry and later owned my own construction company. My hands grasped blueprints and plans for projects that scaled from $400,000 endeavors to colossal undertakings like the 1.5-billion-dollar capital improvement program. This was an era when the scale and complexity of my work painted a vivid picture of capability and ambition. However, life has a curious way of reshuffling our cards, often leading us to avenues we hadn't previously contemplated.

Recognizing an unmet need in the industry, my direction shifted from project management to construction final cleaning. You will hear me say this several times in this book because I want you to realize the importance of an unexpected turn in your life—one that will have a great impact.

Now, for the uninitiated, this might sound like a step-down. But as I looked deeper, I realized the absolute indispensability of this niche. No construction project, regardless of its magnitude or grandeur, can cross the finish line without final cleaning. It's the last, but by no means the least, piece of the puzzle. It's the final touch that transforms a construction site into a finished product ready for its inhabitants.

Yet, it's startling how often we face condescension or underestimation. Certain quarters perceived our new focus as lesser, perhaps even that it really doesn't have that much purpose. But those in the know, those who've felt the pressure of a project's culmination, recognize our role's critical. They understand that we're not just cleaners; we're the seal of completion, the assurance that a project is ready in every sense of the word.

It's a humbling reminder that every role, no matter how seemingly small, has its unique value and significance. Furthermore, the judgments cast upon us were not just about misunderstanding our role but also about not recognizing the vast reservoir of experience and knowledge we brought to the table. They didn't see the project manager with a rich portfolio; they saw just the present.

This journey, with its highs and trials, is a testament to divine providence. I've come to believe that every twist and turn, every decision to embrace a new path, was divinely ordained. There's a certain solace in knowing that a higher power is guiding your steps, ensuring that even when the path seems uncertain, it leads to purpose and fulfillment.

So, the next time you meet someone, be it in construction or any other field, take a moment and pause before you assume. Learn their history and their journey, and you might find a narrative as rich, varied, and inspiring as any epic you've ever read… and remember that every individual's journey, like the most intricate buildings constructed, deserves appreciation, not just for its facade but for the depth and foundation that lie beneath it.

Chapter 16
Embracing Self-Care In The Hustle

In the bustling corridors of our lives, we often find ourselves entangled in the spider web of commitments. For some, it's the relentless pursuit of a flourishing career; for others, it's the ongoing responsibility towards our family. In this spiraling whirlwind, we tend to place ourselves at the bottom of our priority list, especially when the sounds of hammers and drills, like in a construction business, drown the gentle whispers of our inner needs.

There's a saying, "The cobbler's children have no shoes." In the modern context, this means that professionals often neglect their own needs. Such is the irony of life for many entrepreneurs and business owners. As the head of a construction company, I feel that this sentiment resonates all too well.

Days transform into weeks, weeks into months, and before we know it, years have passed, leaving behind a trail of neglected gym memberships, skipped medical appointments, and untaken vacations. We tell ourselves, "I'll hit the gym tomorrow" or "Next week, for sure." But those tomorrows and next week's blend into a mirage that seems constantly out of reach.

However, an epiphany awaits those willing to listen. The realization that, in the grand symphony of life, our well-being isn't just another note; it's the very rhythm that drives the melody. In my case, I had shelved my physical well-being for so long that the weight of neglect began to burden my spirit.

I am paying for that gym membership, but it's not about the money. It's about an investment – an investment in oneself- an affirmation that I am worthy of the time, energy, and resources to be the best version of myself. And as the Word of God clarifies, our prosperity in life is intimately tied to the wellness of our soul. "He wants us to prosper as our souls prosper."

So, why the hesitation? Why the delay? It's time to take the plunge, not out of obligation but out of realization. A realization that in taking care of ourselves, we aren't being selfish. Quite the contrary, we are equipping ourselves to serve those around us better, be it our family, employees, or community. A healthy body houses a vibrant soul; a vibrant soul is a beacon of light to the world.

Starting today, I make a pact with myself: no more deferring or postponing. The gym isn't just a place to build muscles; it's a temple where I reaffirm my commitment to my well-being, where every drop of sweat is a testament to my dedication, and this journey isn't transient; it's a lifelong commitment.

In the backdrop of our careers and commitments, let's keep sight of the bigger picture. Our health, spirit, and faith are the cornerstones upon which the clarity of our life stands. Let's cherish them, nourish them, and celebrate them.

In embracing self-care, we aren't just paving the way for a healthier self but also heralding the dawn of the next level of celebration in life. Because true prosperity, as they say, begins from within.

Chapter 17
Nurturing the Self-Bound by Ambition

Pursuing dreams, no matter how fulfilling, often comes at a price. For many, that price is their well-being. Whether spearheading your own enterprise or navigating the tight ropes of a dream career, the happiness of ambition can sometimes obscure the simple joys and essential rituals of self-care.

On a personal note, life has sometimes been challenging. While the glimmer of ambition lights up the night, the course remains with challenges and obstacles. Yet, through this odyssey of dreams, one lesson emerged clear and resounding: taking care of oneself isn't an indulgence; it's a necessity.

Stress, as we all know, is an omnipresent shadow. In the high-stakes arena of business or any intense profession, it's a rite of passage. But here's a revelation - stress isn't a marker of success; how you manage it is.

I've absorbed a few life lessons to live as stress-free as possible; often, a stress-free life isn't easy. Simple as they may sound, their impact on mental well-being is profound:

Gratitude Over Gloom

Even on the worst days, there's always something to be grateful for. Maybe it's the team that supports you, the family that stands by you, or even the tiny achievements that remind you of your journey. Gratefulness is a powerful antidote to stress and negativity.

The Golden Rule

Treat others as we wish to be treated. This timeless wisdom holds immense power. It's easy to get embroiled in transactional interactions in the corporate realm or any workplace. However, anchoring interactions with empathy and respect elevates our spirit and fosters an environment of mutual respect.

Yet, reality isn't rosy; sometimes, despite our best intentions, we encounter individuals or situations that fail to reciprocate the same kindness. It's disheartening, but it's also a test of our character. The true essence of the Golden Rule isn't in its reciprocity; it's in our steadfastness to the principle, irrespective of the outcome.

Boundaries are Sacred

In the dizzying dance of ambition, it's easy to blur the lines between personal and professional, rest and work, self-time and team time. Drawing clear boundaries isn't selfish. It's an assertion of self-worth and that while ambition is dear, self-care isn't negotiable.

Embrace the Pause

In our relentless rush, we often forget the magic of stillness. Sometimes, it's essential to step back, breathe, and recalibrate. In these pauses, we connect with our inner selves, gain clarity, and rejuvenate our spirits.

Reflecting on this journey, its ebbs and flows, its highs and inevitable lows, there's a quiet acknowledgment. Success isn't merely the milestones achieved or the accolades garnered; it's also about the harmony of the journey, the balance of ambition and well-being, and the ability to stand tall, not just in strength but also in spirit.

Remember, as we chase dreams, let's remember to live the dream. After all, the tapestry of life isn't just threaded with achievements but also strands of self-love, kindness, and gratitude.

Chapter 18
Finding Structure in Chaos

The vast expanse of a construction site, its sprawling infrastructure, the noise of machines, and the synchronized dance of workers is a sight to behold. It might seem like organized chaos to an outsider, but to us, every brick, beam, and bolt has a story and purpose.

However, like every story, there are plot twists, some predictable, others unexpected.

On one of those days, as the sun painted golden hues over the site, I found myself in an unexpected twist. Our team, dedicated to the final construction cleaning, is like the last line of defense before a battlefield is declared safe. Our role is not just to clean but to give the finishing touch, the final polish that makes a structure into a home, an office, a space ready for its purpose.

In a well-structured world, every preceding team would finish their task, and we would step in, ensuring the place sparkles, left without construction residue. However, as I've learned, reality often deviates from the ideal.

Being shuffled around like chess pieces on a board isn't new to us. One floor today, another tomorrow, without the satisfaction of seeing one completed. But on this particular day, the inconsistency reached a peak. Unsurprisingly, we were ushered to a new floor; a bombshell dropped – a floor we were pulled from was being handed over to the owner, and another floor, untouched by us, was scheduled for a handover the following week.

The swirling dust wasn't just around me; it seemed like my vision was clouded by it. I could feel the simmering frustration reaching its boiling point. Yes, I had always advocated for maintaining composure, for standing one's ground without losing one's cool. But, at that moment, the dam broke.

The sarcastic retort from the other side, "You're a project manager; you know how it goes," only fueled the fire. "Yes, I do," I shot back, "and this isn't how."

In the heart of the conflict, the questions that tumbled out weren't just outbursts; they were the culmination of months of trying to bring order to chaos. Where, indeed, was the project schedule? The close-out procedure? These weren't just management tools but symbols of professionalism and respect for each team's work.

Looking back, while the confrontation wasn't pleasant, it was necessary. It was a mirror to the management, a reminder that while flexibility is essential in construction, consistency and respect for a process aren't optional.

It also was a lesson for me. Sometimes, in the middle of the concrete and iron, we need to find our steel, our spine. To ensure a strong structure, we must ensure our foundations of professionalism, respect, and communication are rock solid.

The construction journey isn't just about buildings; it's about building relationships, trust, and a shared vision. And for that, every brick, every beam, every bolt, every individual, and every team matters.

Chapter 19
Building Respect: The Overlooked Pillars of Construction

Like a well-orchestrated opera, the construction industry thrives on the harmonious interplay of various sections, each vital in delivering the symphony of a completed structure. Yet, while every note is crucial for the melody, some are often overshadowed, taken for granted or worse, overlooked entirely. Such has been the fate of the final cleaning crew in this vast realm of bricks and beams.

To an uninformed observer, our task might seem mundane. "They're the cleanup crew," they'd say, dismissing us as mere 'maids and butlers.' But the discerning eye knows the value of what we bring to the table. After the sound of hammers and drills fades away, our hands add the final touch, making spaces livable and making construction feel like home.

Morning meetings serve as the pulse check of any construction project. Trades gather strategies discussed and plans laid out. Yet, the glaring absence of the final cleaning crew in these discussions is more than just an oversight; it's symptomatic of a deeper issue of unrecognized importance and respect.

Each day, as we delve into the apartments, we witness firsthand the aftermath left by other trades. Discarded tools, trash, and an overarching presumption of a cleanup service awaiting them highlight the embedded mindset. While every trade has its challenges, ours often goes beyond the physical labor. We battle with the disregard for our profession, the assumption that we're the 'help,' there to erase the traces of the 'real' workers.

Adding to this is the unsettling undercurrent of gender dynamics. In a predominantly male-driven industry, the presence of female leaders, like a rare gem, should be celebrated. Instead, there's an unmistakable undercurrent of chauvinism. It's never overtly spoken, but the silent whispers, the smirks, and the subtle undermining all echo the same sentiment: "What is she doing here?"

The narrative isn't just about gender; it transcends the deeper issue of respect for roles, irrespective of gender. The mindset that dismisses the importance of final cleaning also relegates female leaders to secondary status. It's a two-pronged challenge, battling both professional and gender stereotypes.

In the midst of all this, there's an urgent need for leadership. Authentic leadership isn't about managing from afar; it's about being in the trenches, understanding the significance, and ensuring every voice is heard and every role acknowledged. Leadership needs to recognize the importance of every wheel in the machine and the value of every hand contributing to the vision.

As we navigate this maze of biases and disregard, there's an imperative for change. It begins with awareness, progresses with dialogue, and ends in action. Construction isn't just about erecting structures; it's about constructing a culture of respect, acknowledgment, and appreciation.

Every brick, bolt, brush stroke, and cleaning swipe matters, and as the industry evolves, it's time to shed outdated biases and build foundations grounded in respect and recognition.

Conclusion

As we reach the final pages of "Be Aware of the Footprints You Leave Behind: The Next Celebration," it is imperative to reflect on the profound journey we have traveled together. This book is more than just a collection of stories; it is a testament to the strength and tenacity of women in the construction industry—a realm traditionally dominated by men.

The narratives shared within these pages highlight the numerous challenges faced by women in construction. From breaking through glass ceilings to overcoming prejudice and bias, these women have demonstrated an unwavering commitment to their craft. Their journeys are a vivid reminder that change is not only possible but essential.

In celebrating these remarkable achievements, we must also acknowledge the work that remains. The construction industry stands at a pivotal juncture, one where the demand for diversity, equity, and inclusion is louder than ever. It is our collective responsibility to ensure that the footprints we leave behind are ones of progress and respect, paving the way for future generations of women to thrive without encountering the same barriers.

This call to action is for everyone—men and women alike. It is about fostering an environment where respect is not earned through struggle but given as a fundamental right. It is about recognizing that diversity in the workforce leads to richer ideas, stronger teams, and more innovative solutions. It is about creating a culture where every woman in construction feels valued, supported, and empowered to reach her full potential.

Let this book be a catalyst for change, a source of inspiration for those who seek to challenge the status quo, and a beacon of hope for women aspiring to carve out their own paths in construction. The next celebration is not just a recognition of what has been achieved but a commitment to what can be accomplished when we stand together, united in our pursuit of equality and respect.

As we move forward, let us be ever mindful of the footprints we leave behind. Let them be imprints of courage, unity, and transformation—footprints that lead us toward a more inclusive and respectful industry. This is our time to build not just structures but a legacy of change. Together, we can construct a future where the celebration of women's contributions in construction is no longer the exception but the norm.

Thank you for joining me on this journey. Let us continue to inspire, build, and celebrate the remarkable women in construction now and always.

About the Author

Meet Angela Boone, a seasoned author, speaker, and entrepreneur with over 40 years of experience. Angela has worked on projects ranging from $400K to a $1.5 Billion capital improvement program.

Angela has been featured in several local, national, and international publications, such as the cover of Michigan Contractors and Builders magazine, in which she was a contributing writer. She was featured in the "Voice" a British magazine, and she was featured in Essence, under the title, Making It Happen, Creating Success and Abundance, and also in Essences, under the title, Wealth and Work, "How I did it".

There have been dozens of awards and articles published on Angela's success as a business leader in the community and as an author and mentor—featured in the Detroit News and

Free Press, Front Page, Michigan Chronicle, Crain's Detroit Business, and more. Numerous radio and television interviews have taken place on several Detroit area talk shows, both nationally and internationally. In 2004, she was a guest on WGBB 1240 A.M. in New York on the radio show: "Word Up Gospel"; WNOO radio in Florida, WXTC Heaven 1390 and "Premier Christian Radio" in London, England, just to name a few.

Boone attended Lawrence Technical University in Southfield, Michigan School of Engineering, where she studied Civil Engineering course work; the International Academy of Design and Technology, where she studied Interior Design; and Colorado Technical University, where she received her associate degree in Business Administration.

As a project engineer who gained experience in project management and general contracting while working for a well-known contractor. Learn

more at www.ARBooneConstruction.com

www.ingramcontent.com/pod-product-compliance
Lightning Source LLC
Chambersburg PA
CBHW071943210526
45479CB00002B/798